A NOTE TO PARENTS

When your children are ready to "step into reading," giving them the right books is as crucial as giving them the right food to eat. **Step into Reading Books** present exciting stories and information reinforced with lively, colorful illustrations that make learning to read fun, satisfying, and worthwhile. They are priced so that acquiring an entire library of them is affordable. And they are beginning readers with a difference—they're written on five levels.

Early Step into Reading Books are designed for brand-new readers, with large type and only one or two lines of very simple text per page. **Step 1 Books** feature the same easy-to-read type as the Early Step into Reading Books, but with more words per page. **Step 2 Books** are both longer and slightly more difficult, while **Step 3 Books** introduce readers to paragraphs and fully developed plot lines. **Step 4 Books** offer exciting nonfiction for the increasingly independent reader.

The grade levels assigned to the five steps—preschool through kindergarten for the Early Books, preschool through grade 1 for Step 1, grades 1 through 3 for Step 2, grades 2 through 3 for Step 3, and grades 2 through 4 for Step 4—are intended only as guides. Some children move through all five steps very rapidly; others climb the steps over a period of several years. Either way, these books will help your child "step into reading" in style!

To Reed, and all the kids of Mrs. Block's 1997 class.

—S.A.K.

Cover photo credits: Reuters/John Kuntz/Archive Photos; J. D. Cuban/Allsport;
John Burgess/*Sports Illustrated.*

Text photo credits: Seth Poppel Yearbook Archives, p. 4; Seth Poppel Yearbook Archives, p. 17;
J. D. Cuban/Allsport, p. 27; Reuters/Mike Blake/Archive Photos, p. 31; Craig Jones/Allsport, p. 38;
Steve Munday/Allsport, p. 45; AP Photo/Kathy Willens, p. 48.

http://www.randomhouse.com/

Library of Congress Cataloging-in-Publication Data
Kramer, Sydelle.
Tiger Woods, golf's young master / by S. A. Kramer ; illustrated with photographs. p.   cm.
(Step into reading. A Step 4 book.) SUMMARY: A biography of the youngest player, and the
first person of color, ever to win the Masters Golf Tournament.
ISBN 0-679-88849-7 (pbk). — ISBN 0-679-98849-1 (lib. bdg.).
1. Woods, Tiger—Juvenile literature. 2. Golfers—United States—Biography—Juvenile literature.
3. Racially mixed people—United States—Biography—Juvenile literature.
[1. Woods, Tiger. 2. Golfers. 3. Racially mixed people—Biography.]
I. Title. II. Series: Step into reading. Step 4 book.
GV964.W66K73 1998   796.352'092—dc21   97-36672

Printed in the United States of America   10 9 8 7 6 5 4 3 2

STEP INTO READING is a registered trademark of Random House, Inc.

Step into Reading®

TIGER WOODS

GOLF'S YOUNG MASTER

By S. A. Kramer

A Step 4 Book

Random House 🏠 New York

Tiger's high school yearbook photo.
Fellow students voted him "most likely to succeed."

1
GOLFING IN DIAPERS

Tiger Woods seemed in a hurry to be born. He arrived on December 30, 1975, as though he couldn't wait for the new year to begin. His mom, Kutilda, named him Eldrick. But his dad, Earl, called him Tiger. Tiger had been the nickname of Earl's best friend, a soldier who had saved Earl's life in battle.

Earl and Tida (TEE-dah), as Kutilda was called, lived in Cypress, California. Earl was a retired army officer who worked for a company that built rockets. He is a quarter Native American, a quarter Chinese, and half black.

Tida was born in Thailand, a country in Asia. She is a quarter Chinese, a quarter white, and half Thai. When Tiger was born, Tida stayed home to raise him. He was the Woodses' only child, the center of their lives.

From the time Tiger was born, Earl had a feeling he would be athletic. Earl himself was an excellent golfer. And he knew that the earlier a child learns a sport, the better he or she will be as an adult.

So when Tiger was just six months old, Earl carried him to the garage. That was where Earl practiced, stroking ball after ball into a net. He strapped Tiger into his highchair, grabbed a club, and started swinging.

For four months, Earl practiced and Tiger watched. Then one day, Tiger climbed down from his highchair. He couldn't walk yet, but he snatched a plastic putter (a kind of club). Eyeing the ball, he got set, then swung smoothly. *Whack!* His shot sailed right into the net! Earl couldn't believe it. He ran and got Tida. As both parents watched, Tiger did it again.

There and then, the Woodses made a plan. They would give Tiger every chance he needed to develop his talent. But they would never *force* him to play or practice. If Tiger was to succeed at the game, he had to love golf for himself.

He did. At the age of two, he won his first tournament—wearing diapers! He used sawed-off clubs, since regular ones were taller than he was. He was so eager to play that he'd call Earl at work and ask, "Daddy, can I practice with you today?"

When Tiger was almost three, a television talk show did a story on him. Smiling for the cameras, he teed off (hit the first stroke of a hole off a two-inch wooden peg in the ground) beautifully. Then he out-putted the famous guests.

Tiger learned the game fast. Soon he was able to select the right club for each of his shots (there are fourteen clubs in every golf bag). He also stroked his first *birdie*. (Each hole allows a fixed number of strokes to get the ball in the cup. That fixed number is called *par*. Shooting one stroke under par is a birdie.)

By the age of four, Tiger had a professional coach. By five, he'd appeared on another TV show. Strangers asked for his autograph.

When he was six, Tiger shot his first hole in one (when the ball goes into the cup in just one stroke). His athletic skill was remarkable. But Earl and Tida knew talent alone wasn't enough to make him a champion. Tiger had to learn to concentrate so hard that not even a herd of elephants could distract him.

Yet how could a first-grader keep his thoughts from wandering? One day, Earl brought home special tapes that contained subliminal messages. Mixed in with soothing music and the sounds of waterfalls, waves, and wind were spoken messages such as "I focus and give it my all!" and "I believe in me!"

The tapes seemed to help Tiger with his concentration and confidence. He liked listening to them. Earl had other ideas, too. He would purposely try to distract Tiger. As the boy got ready to swing, Earl would jingle coins in his pocket. Sometimes he'd rip open the Velcro on his golf glove or drop his golf bag or caw like a crow.

The distractions were hard on Tiger. But they worked. Earl said later, "I wanted to make sure he'd never run into anybody who was tougher mentally than he was."

Tiger's first real test came in the second grade, when he entered an international tournament to play against children from all over the world. Before Tiger teed off, Earl pulled him aside. He said, "Son, I want you to know I love you no matter how you do. Enjoy yourself."

That's what Tiger did. His first shot was a perfect drive. Completely relaxed, he easily finished first.

It was only the beginning. At the age of eight, he won the Optimist International World Junior Championship (a title he would win five more times). By the time he was eleven, he was undefeated in over thirty statewide events. Earl and Tida were very proud.

They were devoted to Tiger. Borrowing thousands of dollars, they got him the best equipment and coaches. They also made sure Tiger had fun. He watched football and wrestling, played video games, and went to the movies. There wasn't a roller coaster around he didn't ride. His favorite music was rap, and he loved to blast it on his radio.

But Earl and Tida didn't spoil him. Tida insisted he have good manners. Tiger was not allowed to lose his temper, even when he made a bad shot. At a young age, he learned about responsibility. Tida said, "If he didn't finish his homework, I wouldn't take him to the golf course."

Tiger knew school was important. But nothing made him feel as good as golf. He wanted to be the best ever—better even than Jack Nicklaus, golf's greatest player.

But Earl and Tida realized Tiger was up against more than Nicklaus had ever been. Nicklaus was white. Tiger was black and Asian. It was the 1980s, but a person of color had never been a golfing superstar.

Golf first started over five hundred years ago in Scotland. It didn't cross the ocean to America until 1888. For years, it wasn't especially popular. Almost all golf courses belonged to private clubs. Most charged a lot of money to join. They did not accept people of color, or women, as members.

Golf was a white man's sport. It wasn't until 1975 that a black athlete appeared in America's most important golfing event, the Masters. Players of color were so rare that people sometimes stared at Tiger when he practiced.

But Tiger was convinced his color didn't matter. If he mastered every stroke, golf's doors would swing open. So by the age of twelve, he'd learned to smash tremendous drives. His approach shots from the fairway to the green were steady, and his short putts always found the cup. He had a way of making winning look easy.

Still, he would get nervous. The night before an event, he'd eat and eat, then eat some more. He'd shake so hard in the shower, he'd drop the soap.

Despite all his training, his concentration could be poor. He often started a game slowly, as though he had to warm up, like a car. Although he never rushed his shots, now and then he would slash a wild one. The ball would zoom off the fairway (the wide, open lawn that starts off each hole). Out of control, it would land in the rough (tall grass, rocks, and bushes) or a bunker (a long dent in the grass filled with sand) or a water hazard (a pond or stream).

Tiger would get furious with himself. Then, on the very next shot, he'd snap off a perfect drive. Often he'd cheer for himself, and his whole mood would change.

Behind his warm brown eyes and friendly face, Tiger was steely in his will to win. By the time he was fourteen, the Woodses' living room was jammed with trophies. He was growing up fast.

2
THE BUZZ BEGINS

It was the summer of 1990. Tiger's game was going well. With his slim, muscular body, Tiger moved gracefully over the course. Fans loved his good looks and neat appearance. His clothes never seemed wrinkled. Even his golf shoes looked clean!

Fourteen-year-old Tiger played in all the important tournaments. He won event after event. By September, he was exhausted.

Sports agents began phoning. Even the pros were taking notice. One called him "awesome." But Tiger didn't let the fuss get to him. He told reporters, "I'm glad to get back in school and be with my friends."

It was his first year in high school, and

Tiger wanted to do well. He earned close to straight A's. But he didn't stop playing golf. He was on the school team.

Then, when he was fifteen, the buzz got louder. *Sports Illustrated* ran a story on him. In it, Tiger said he shouldn't be labeled according to race. "I don't want to be the best black golfer on the Tour. I want to be the best *golfer* on the Tour," he said.

Some experts thought Tiger was getting ahead of himself. On occasion, he still played like a kid. He'd swing too hard and not place the ball properly. He said he was "icy under pressure," but his emotions still clouded his thinking sometimes. Instead of taking safe shots, he took unnecessary chances.

Mistakes almost cost Tiger the 1991 U.S. Junior Amateur Championship. The last round (eighteen holes) was held on July 28 in Orlando, Florida. After just six holes, Tiger was three strokes down. Many golfers would have folded. But Tiger had inner strength.

With his never-give-up style, he staged a comeback. By the end of the round, he was tied for the lead. There had to be a playoff to decide the winner. (In golf, a playoff has no time limit. The tournament isn't over until one golfer reaches the cup in fewer strokes than the other.)

Tiger felt confident. He was playing in what he called the "zone." In the zone, he thought with his body, not his mind. His instincts helped him choose a club and make a great shot.

Tiger won the tournament on the very first playoff hole. He became the youngest golfer—and first person of color—ever to win the Junior Am. But he was so tired afterward that he couldn't even talk.

Suddenly, everyone was talking about Tiger Woods. He was the youngest golfer ever to be named the American Junior Golf Association's Player of the Year. Experts started to compare him to Jack Nicklaus.

In February 1992, Tiger became the youngest player in history to appear in a PGA (Professional Golf Association) tournament. He was only in his second year of high school, yet he was golfing with the pros. But unlike them, he had to get permission to miss school in order to play!

Fans crowded courses to see him. They loved it when they caught a glimpse of his golf bag. His driver (the club used to tee off

Tiger poses with his school's varsity golf team.

WESTERN HIGH SCHOOL

with) had a cover that looked like a tiger. Tida had made it. On it she had stitched "Love from Mom" in Thai.

Tiger was a crowd-pleaser. But he was also a champion. In the summer of 1992, he won another Junior Am title. It was the first time a golfer had ever won it twice.

Instead of relaxing, Tiger played in more tournaments. Soon he was exhausted. Friends called, but he was too tired to go out. In his spare time, he rested in his room.

Tiger couldn't gain weight. He was seventeen years old and six foot one, but he weighed only 140 pounds. So he stuffed himself at McDonald's. He'd eat seven slices of pizza in one meal. But not even strawberry milk shakes and vanilla ice cream cones could beef him up. The strain of his hectic life was beginning to show.

Things seemed to get better in 1993. The magazine *Golf World* named Tiger its 1992 Player of the Year. He never missed a practice, and he still got A's and B's in school. With a girlfriend and a car, he had an active social life. But everything came crashing to a halt in June. Tiger came down with mononucleosis, a bad virus. It left him so weak and tired that he couldn't pick up a club for three weeks, but he recovered just in time for the 1993 Junior Am.

The tournament was held in Portland, Oregon. A record crowd turned out for the final round. Fans knew that if Tiger won three titles in a row, it would be a golfing first.

Before he teed off, Tiger stretched to relax his muscles. Then he put a white glove on his left hand. His right hand was bare. The crowd could see a strip of white tape neatly wound around his middle finger.

To check the wind's direction, Tiger pulled up a clump of grass, threw it in the air, and watched where it blew. Then, gripping his driver, he hooked his right pinky under the second finger of his left hand. He swung fast and hard. Fans heard the club whir through the air. There was a crack, and bits of grass and dirt were kicked high. The ball zoomed down the fairway.

The gallery (a golf crowd) clapped and cheered. They kept it up at every hole. Even when Tiger hit a bad shot, they applauded.

By the eighteenth hole, Tiger was behind by one stroke. He knew he'd have to do better than par the hole. To tie, he'd have to birdie it.

Par was five. Tiger slammed his first shot more than 300 yards. But it landed in the rough by the side of the fairway. His second shot slapped down forty yards from the green (the grassy area around the cup)— right into a bunker.

Two strokes left for a birdie. To get near the cup, Tiger would have to make a long bunker shot, one of golf's hardest. Many in the crowd thought he was through.

They didn't know Tiger. Lashing his club

around, he pounded the ball out of the sand. It landed ten feet from the hole.

A hush spread over the gallery. Tiger removed his glove and stuffed it in his back pocket. Clutching his putter barehanded, he took two practice swings. Then he looked at the hole, at the ball, at the hole again, and at the ball. Finally, he put his head down, spread his feet apart, and straightened his legs.

The inch-and-a-half ball seemed so tiny. It weighed just an ounce and a half—so easy to hit too hard. The cup itself was only four inches deep and four and a quarter inches wide. Gently, Tiger swung his putter. The ball rolled toward the hole...and dipped in! Birdie! The gallery went wild.

Now the tournament was tied. It was play-off time. On the very first hole, Tiger got the victory. Earl raced onto the green. Father and son hugged and cried. "I did it, I did it," Tiger joyfully declared.

3
YEAR OF THE TIGER

In the spring of 1994, Tiger graduated from high school. With his close-to-A average, he won the Dial Award as America's top scholar-athlete. That fall, he would attend Stanford University on a full scholarship.

But first, there was a summer of golf. Tiger was playing better than ever. He'd learned not to use all his power, to make his swing slower and tighter. From start to finish, it made a complete circle. Experts watching him thought he had perfect form.

His swing was graceful and smooth, and it packed a punch. The ball would rocket high and long down the fairway. One pro said,

"It's hard to believe anybody hits the ball that far."

But when Tiger finished the stroke, he looked as if he'd been in an accident! His right foot had turned with his body, sliding up on its toes. Yet his left foot had stayed put, as though it were glued to the ground. Each foot headed in a different direction.

Tiger studied the game hard. He'd learned to pay attention to the weather. Was it a clear, sunny day? Then the ball would shoot off the tee like a bullet. Was it damp and humid? Then the ball would feel heavy.

When it rained, the ball wouldn't skip much on the grass. But if it were dry, the ball would bounce as if it were on a trampoline.

Hot weather slowed the ball down; cool weather sped it up. A strong wind could blow it around like a kite.

With all he had learned, Tiger felt ready for the 1994 U.S. Amateur. If he placed first, he'd be the only golfer ever to win both the Amateur and the Junior Am. At eighteen years old, he'd be the youngest Amateur champ ever. No black or Asian-American man had won it before.

The Amateur began on August 25, 1994, in Ponte Vedra Beach, Florida. No one could miss the determined look on Tiger's face. He easily qualified for the final round.

It was hot and humid on the links. Dragonflies and mosquitoes buzzed around the golfers. Tiger was dressed for the heat in shorts and a red-and-white polo shirt. His white shoes and socks gleamed in the sun.

The final round was thirty-six holes. From the start, Tiger was behind, down by six after thirteen holes. No one had ever come from so far back to win the Amateur.

During the lunch break, Tiger showered and changed his clothes. It gave him the feeling he was making a new start. As the afternoon round began, Earl whispered in Tiger's ear, "Let the legend grow."

Somewhere inside him, Tiger knew he could pull it off, and sure enough, by the sixteenth hole, he had tied the game.

The seventeenth hole was dangerous. Tiger knew he could win or lose the title there. Nicknamed the "Island Hole," it had a short fairway and a green surrounded by water. A bad shot would put the ball smack into the pond.

Tiger decided to take a gamble. He'd try to hit the ball all the way to the green in just one stroke. If he made it, he'd have a chance for a birdie. But if he didn't, he'd lose the tournament.

The crowd grew quiet. At home in California, Tida watched on TV. She was so nervous, her heart was pounding.

With his quick, strong hands, Tiger bashed the ball off the tee. It flew high as a bird over the water. When it came down, it took one hop on the green. Then it spun back a little and stopped three feet from the pond's edge.

The shot had worked! Tida couldn't believe it. She rolled off the bed and onto the floor. "That boy almost gave me a heart attack," she said later. "All I kept saying was, 'God, don't let that ball go in the water.'"

But Tiger hadn't won the hole yet. There was a fourteen-foot putt to sink. He studied the grass and the tilt of the green. Then, very calmly, he hit the ball. As it rolled to the cup, his mouth fell open.

Birdie! Tiger kicked up his left foot and slugged the air with his right arm. He had the lead now, and he wouldn't give it up.

The title was his. The greatest comeback in the history of the Amateur was complete. A tearful Earl told his son, "You have done something no black person has ever done, and you will forever be a part of history."

It seemed as if everyone wanted to congratulate Tiger. Jesse Jackson called him. Television talk shows invited him to appear. His hometown gave him the key to the city.

Tiger Woods had arrived.

Victory! *Tiger wins the 1994 U.S. Amateur.*

4
THREE-PEAT

After the Amateur, Tiger started college. Busier than ever, he studied hard and played for Stanford's golf team. But he also made sure he had fun, attending every party he could. He relaxed by biking sixty miles along the California coast.

His life was going well. *Golf World* named him its 1994 Man of the Year. The *Los Angeles Times* gave him its 1994 Player of the Year award. And winning the Amateur meant he could play in his first Masters. Nineteen-year-old Tiger would be competing against the best.

Each year, the Masters is held at the Augusta National Golf Club in Augusta,

Georgia. The course there is famous for its slick greens. A putt that is accurate anywhere else can skid right by the cup there.

The Masters started on April 6, 1995. As Tiger entered the clubhouse, he felt the past all around him. The greatest golfers had all been victorious here, winning the green jacket that's awarded instead of a trophy.

It was a tournament of champions. Yet for years, it had been an American disgrace. Tiger knew it wasn't long ago that blacks weren't welcome here.

Tiger was the first black amateur to ever play in the Masters. In sixty-one years, only three other black golfers had walked these links. No black man had played here since 1988. The club itself had admitted no black members until 1990.

At the Masters, Tiger made history with every stroke. Even though he lost, he wasn't disappointed. No one knew better than Tiger himself that he was still learning the game.

As soon as the tournament was over, Tiger hurried back to Stanford. The next morning, he had a history final. It wasn't easy playing golf and being a student.

In September, he won his second consecutive U.S. Amateur and started his second year at Stanford. His schedule became more and more hectic. Always on the run, Tiger didn't even have time for a girlfriend.

He got exhausted again. He started missing classes. His grades slipped. Even his golf game suffered. He made bad shots and lost his temper, smacking his bag and throwing his clubs.

It seemed as if Tiger was trying to do too much. Something had to give, and Tiger knew it.

By the summer of 1996, he was thinking of becoming a professional golfer. If he left college and turned pro, he could earn a lot of money. There'd be no more cramming for exams and trying to win tournaments at the

His first Masters. While Tiger had fun at the Masters, he didn't yet have the experience to win.

same time. Playing the pros would be the supreme challenge.

Before he made up his mind, Tiger wanted to enter one more tournament—the 1996 U.S. Amateur. If he won, he'd have three Amateur victories in a row. No one had ever "three-peated" the Amateur.

In August, Tiger arrived at the Pumpkin Ridge Golf Club in Cornelius, Oregon. Fifteen thousand fans were there to greet him. Over the next few days, he shot six beautiful rounds to qualify for Sunday's final.

That morning had a special feel to it. Something was happening to golf, and it was because of Tiger. People who had never followed the game before were now eager to watch it. Even little kids were showing up to see him play.

Now six foot two, Tiger swung faster and harder than anyone else. His long legs and quick shoulders helped him pound the ball up to 380 yards. That's three times longer than a major-league home run!

The gallery oohed and aahed and kept their eyes glued on Tiger. He was easy to spot—he was wearing a red shirt. When Tiger dresses in red, he's going for victory.

Fans leaned out to touch him, shake his hand, and cheer him on. They shouted "Kill 'em, Tiger!" or "You go, T!" He was asked to autograph everything from hats to score-cards. Ever polite, he often responded, "No problem."

He'd high-five kids and throw them balls he wasn't going to use. In the midst of applause, he'd thank fans for rooting him on. He'd even share a joke with them.

But it didn't look as if he was going to pull out a win. After the first twenty holes, he was five strokes down. Then all of a sudden, he got down to work. With his tremendous will to win, he finished the round in a tie.

It was playoff time. The game came down to the thirty-eighth hole. Only Tiger made par. The championship was his!

Twenty-year-old Tiger threw his arms into the air. He had just become the greatest amateur golfer ever.

5
THE PRO

Three days later, Tiger flew to Milwaukee, Wisconsin. With Earl beside him, he spoke to reporters. He had made up his mind—he was turning pro. As photographers snapped his picture, he explained he wasn't doing it for the money. "It was about happiness," he said.

Tiger also wanted to open up golf to people of color. As the first black or Asian with a chance to be number one, Tiger felt he'd bring people of color to the links. As a superstar, he could help shape the game into a truly American sport.

Tiger's announcement was big news. Before he'd even played a shot as a pro, he was asked to endorse products. He ended up signing deals worth over sixty million dollars. Overnight, Tiger became a millionaire.

But many of the pros didn't take him seriously. To them, he was still just a kid. Some didn't think he'd even make the PGA tour. (A golfer can't just enter the PGA events he wants to—he has to qualify for them.)

Tiger, though, had confidence in himself. So did the fans. They came out to see him in record numbers. At his first pro tournament, twenty thousand people stood six rows deep. Tida joked, "The only way to watch my Tiger now is on TV."

By his third event, there were a hundred thousand people in the gallery. The fourth was a sell-out, and almost a mob scene! Hordes of fans darted about, climbing buildings and rocks for the chance to catch a glimpse of Tiger.

All kinds of people were coming to see him—Asian and black, Latino and white, young and old, male and female. Chanting

"Ti-ger, Ti-ger," they treated him like an idol. Reporters began calling PGA events "the Tiger Tour."

The noisy galleries would have bothered some players. Not Tiger. He laughed, "If you lose a ball, there are a lot of people out there to help you find it."

Tiger was having fun. Still, there were days he got lonely. The other players on the tour were much older than he was. With no one to talk to, he missed college and his friends. He longed to go "to a buddy's house or a dorm at eleven at night and just hang out."

More than ever, golf was Tiger's life. He rarely skipped practice. Even in the rain, he'd be out on the driving range. But he hadn't yet won a professional tournament.

In October 1996, he flew to Nevada. The world's top golfers were playing in the Las Vegas Invitational. It would be a tough field to beat, but Tiger badly wanted a win.

From his penthouse hotel suite, he had a great view of Las Vegas. There was a TV in every room, and a private elevator that only he could use. Tiger was getting the star treatment, and he wanted to show the pros he deserved it.

It looked as if he would have to wait. Before the final round, Tiger was four strokes down. To make things worse, he was limping from a pulled muscle. But the pain seemed to make him more determined. After eighteen holes, he was tied for the lead.

For the first time as a professional, Tiger was in a playoff. He went to the practice tee and calmly hit a few shots. Then he ate a banana for energy.

Tiger was on his game. The playoff was over fast. As fans screamed his name, he triumphed on the first hole.

After the victory, Tiger got into a stretch

Hole in one! *Tiger at the 1997 Phoenix Open.*

limousine. That night he celebrated his first professional victory with a special dinner. Sipping champagne, he downed two Mc-Donald's cheeseburgers.

Two weeks later, he won the Disney Classic. It was his second triumph in his first seven pro events—the greatest professional start in golf history.

By the end of 1996, he'd had the most remarkable rookie season of all time. *Sports*

Illustrated named him Sportsman of the Year. Only twenty-one, he was the youngest athlete ever to earn the honor. He was also voted PGA Rookie of the Year.

In 1997, he didn't let up. The year's first pro event was the Mercedes Championship in Carlsbad, California. The weather was miserable. The rain wouldn't stop, but neither would Tiger. He took home the title, along with a brand-new Mercedes.

Three wins in nine appearances! Prize money of over a million dollars! No one had ever won so much so fast on the PGA tour. But Tiger didn't seem surprised. Winning, he told reporters, "is what I set out to do."

There seemed to be no stopping him.

6
THE GREEN JACKET

April 10, 1997. Augusta, Georgia. It was the opening round of the sixty-first Masters. More than any other event, Tiger wanted to win this one. He'd have to beat eighty-five golfers for the first prize of $486,000 and the honor of wearing the green jacket.

Some experts thought Tiger had a good chance. No one else clobbered the ball as far or controlled the speed of his putts as well. But others felt he was a long shot. After all, he hadn't yet won a major tournament, and he'd played in Augusta just twice before. Only those who knew the course well had ever won.

Tiger realized he had something to prove. He knew there were people who felt his talent was mostly hype. But if he finished first here, everyone would know he was for real.

No one as young as he was had ever won the Masters before. No person of color had ever worn the green jacket. The odds were against Tiger. Could he prove them wrong?

The fans thought so. As he got ready to tee off, the largest gallery ever to see a Masters first round cheered him on. It was so hard to get a ticket, a pass to see every one of the tournament rounds was sold illegally for $10,000!

Tiger was a little nervous. By the time he was halfway through the round, he had bogeyed four holes. (A bogey is one stroke over par.) Some fans wondered if the cool air was bothering him. After all, the temperature was only forty-three degrees. A chill wind was blowing up to twenty miles per hour.

But Tiger knew his problem wasn't the weather. It was his swing. At the tenth hole, he suddenly realized he had to shorten it. Tiger birdied the tenth. But now he had to play the next three holes. Called the Amen Corner, they are among the hardest in golf. Their beautiful flowering trees and bushes stand near deep bunkers and long hazards. The Amen Corner would be a great test of Tiger's game.

His shortened swing worked. The old smooth stroke clicked in. Tiger parred the eleventh hole, then birdied both the twelfth and thirteenth. By the end of the round, he was only three strokes off the lead.

The next day, he was confident. He shot a blazing six under par. And on day three, he was even better. With seven birdies, he had a seven under par. He led the tournament by an amazing nine strokes.

The final round was Sunday. A strong wind flapped the yellow flags on the greens madly. Tiger wore a red shirt. He was dressed for victory.

Despite his big lead, he knew he had to stay focused. Calm as ever, he parred the first hole, then birdied the second. But then he started to feel the pressure. He bogeyed both the fifth hole and the seventh.

All at once, Tiger remembered Earl's advice—play like yourself. His game clicked back in. He birdied the eighth, the eleventh, the thirteenth, and the fourteenth holes. Now he could set a record for the lowest Masters score *ever*. All he had to do was maintain par the rest of the way.

As he walked from hole to hole, the gallery stood and cheered. The ovations were so long, it was as though no one wanted to stop. People reached out and touched him. Grinning widely, Tiger slapped their palms and tipped his hat. But he never stopped thinking about the record.

At last Tiger was playing the eighteenth

and final hole. He took a deep breath and jabbed the tee into the ground. This was it: for the Masters and the history books.

As he teed off, a camera clicked twice, loudly. Caught offguard by the noise, Tiger jerked his swing. The ball hooked left off the fairway as he glared over his shoulder. He spat out one word—"Please."

The next shot was crucial. To get the record, Tiger had to make par. If he didn't hit the ball up on the green, he wouldn't have a chance.

The noisy crowd grew very still. Tiger smacked the ball with his wedge (a kind of club). When it came down, it was just twelve feet from the cup! The gallery cheered. Tiger was beaming.

As he moved to the ball, Tiger remem-bered the black golfers who had come before him—the three professionals who had played here once, and the countless great ones who had been denied. He revealed later, "I said a little prayer of thanks to those guys."

Only two more strokes for par. Tiger's first putt passed by the hole. Miss! But his next, a five-footer, dipped in. Par! He'd taken the Masters and set a record!

The green jacket! *Tiger celebrates after winning the 1997 Masters.*

Tiger punched the air with his right fist. Then he walked off the green to his parents. Tears pouring down his face, he hugged Earl tightly. Tida stroked his arm and wept.

Tiger's achievement left both experts and pros reeling. His eighteen-under-par 270 was the lowest Masters score ever. His nearest opponent was twelve strokes behind. No one had ever had a larger margin of victory.

At twenty-one, Tiger was the youngest Masters winner. He was also the first person of color to wear the green jacket. In fact, he was the only person of color to ever win a major golf championship. And he had accomplished all this as a PGA Tour rookie!

But golfing records weren't the only ones Tiger broke that day. More people watched the Masters on television than ever before. Even the President called to congratulate him.

Tiger had changed golf forever.

7
CONCLUSION

What's next for Tiger? By winning more and more tournaments, he's already set a new record—most money ever earned in a single PGA season. One pro calls him the most important golfer of the last fifty years.

He's proud to be golf's first superstar of color. A role model for kids, he gives golf clinics in cities throughout America. One day in Phoenix, Arizona, 2,500 children showed up!

His millions haven't spoiled him. He still wears his Mickey Mouse watch and eats at McDonald's. Most importantly, he believes in using his money to help others. In January 1997, Tiger started the Tiger Woods Foundation to aid poor children. He may want to be

*At one of his golf clinics, Tiger shows
a boy how to grip a club.*

the world's best golfer, but he also wants to
end prejudice in his sport.

Because of him, a new age has dawned in
golf. It's Tiger Time. If anyone can make the
game a prime-time sport, it's Tiger Woods.